How to Write Erotica:

The Essential Guide to Writing & Publishing Short Erotica that Sells!

Genevieve Marchand

Preface

Writing Erotica has become one of the fastest and easiest ways to make money online.

How to Write Erotica was written with an eye for the for the aspiring Erotica author as an easy-to-use guide for writing your book.

Its practical approach is meant to provide a framework and for understanding just what it takes to write a book of this nature.

In recent years, there's been a fundamental shift from traditional publishing platforms to self- publishing. Now anyone has the opportunity to write and have their book published.

This book is loosely organized into three parts. Chapters 1-8 discusses everything about writing. It covers everything from the tools to the method. Chapters 9 & 10 guide you in how to upload your book to Kindle and CreateSpace. And the final Chapters, 11-21, cover the marketing of your book.

Table of Contents:

Introduction:

I am going to assume that if you picked up this book you are a published Erotica Author or will be one soon. At any rate, you are certainly ahead of the crowd and I want to commend you for it.

I have been writing fervently for the past few years and have been able to build a substantial monthly passive income all generated from my Erotica books.

No longer are writers subject to the frustration of traditional publishing. For that matter, taken out of the equation is the need to work with the traditional publisher altogether.

The writer can determine his/her own fate. More specifically, the author can maintain control of his/her own book. He/ she can retain the rights, control his/ her marketing efforts and receive a greater share of the revenues. With Amazon you can write as many books as you want and take up to seventy percent in royalties.

With the barriers to entry removed all you need is the ability to string a story together that is readable and that is interspersed with some steamy sex scenes. The beautiful part is that if you don't get it right the first time, you can try again.

This simple guide provides authors and publishers with the wisdom that I have gathered while in the trenches of this burgeoning genre. Use its proven techniques to help get your book written, published & discovered.

Good Luck!

Chapter 1: Why Write Erotica?

Since I can remember, I have been fascinated with erotica.

Oddly enough, my first exposure to it was from reading Penthouse Forum. My boyfriend at the time used to sneak Penthouse in the house, and I would pick up the copy while he was at school because my curiosity would just kill me. Needless to say, the next thing I knew was that I enjoyed reading the Forum section. From then on, I started to dabble with writing erotica first for us and then later for Literotica.

Although there may be some drawbacks due to content, this genre has become more wide open in the last decade. Case and point: *Fifty Shades of Grey.*

Just think of how successful *Fifty Shades of Grey* by E.L. James is. Every woman along with a sprinkling of men read that book. I for one read it in one sitting. Imagine having just a bit of E.L. James' new-found wealth!

Bear in mind, there is no shortage of readers out there for this kind of book. In particular, women have flocked to erotic fiction. As a published author catering to this niche you are automatically differentiated from the crowd. Not only does it satisfy a curiosity, it also is gratifying to see your thoughts and fantasies put down in a book for the entertainment of others. Not only that but, customers will generally pay a premium for this type of book if it is well-written, has a decent plot and has some steamy sex.

Lastly, as a society, we embrace books. A book remains the best way to share an idea or story that matters. And if it ignites your curiosity, perhaps it will to the same to others?

Chapter 2: Why Self-Publish?

A "*disruptive technology*" is one that displaces an established technology and shakes up an entire industry or it is a groundbreaking product that creates a completely new industry.

Right before our very eyes, a revolutionary opportunity has emerged for the writer to become his/her own publisher. There is nothing less than a "*digital revolution*" taking place as the e-book and Print-on-Demand has single-handedly disrupted the stagnant sector of publishing and democratized it in the process. Anyone can be a writer.

No longer are writers subject to the frustration of traditional publishing. For that matter, taken out of the equation is the need to work with the traditional publisher altogether! The writer can determine his/her own fate. More specifically, the author can maintain control of his/her own book. He/ she can retain the rights, control his/ her marketing efforts and receive a greater share of the revenues.

Print on Demand (POD) and e-book publishing have created a whole new model for publishing. Are POD and digital books the answer to an author's prayers, or just an evolutionary step between traditional publishing models and free Internet distribution?

As a society, we embrace and value books. We consider them to be excellent sources of information. In other words, a book remains the best way to share an idea or story that matters. And if it matters to you, perhaps it will matter to others?

Granted, writing can be seen as a challenge, but nothing in life that is worth it comes easy, or? It is my firm belief that we all have a book in us just waiting to come out.

Chapter 3: Tools of the Trade

Although I embrace all the technology that abounds, I do for the most part split out how I get my ideas to paper. That is, I like to write longhand with a pen and paper and then type up with a word processor what I have done. Some may say, it is inefficient but to me it acts as a first line edit when I transfer over chapter by chapter.

I do sometimes, however, type straight into the Word, but I am not a fan of staring at screens for long periods. Other times, I dictate into my I phone and then add what I have dictated over into Word. Be watchful, of this method. Although quick, it must be edited as you go. Voice recognition is great but is not there yet.

There are two musts to get you on your way to becoming the next E.L James. These are **Microsoft Word** and **Scrivener**.

Microsoft Word is by far the most common word processing program out there. There is no need to upset the apple cart, so to say. You can get so much done with the entire Microsoft Suite itself, but here I just wanted to mention word.

It is not the word I grew up with. There is hidden functionality all over the place! It is easy, affordable and, most importantly, gets the job done.

Scrivener is great. It's easy to use, easy to keep organized, infinitely flexible, and for those long-term thinkers, you can compile straight to any format, including e-book formats that are ready to publish on

Kindle and various other e-book platforms. There are all sorts of great templates to choose from. For example, it has character and setting sketch templates, it autosaves your work, and it rarely ever crashes (unlike the options above). I could go on for days about Scrivener.

Another tool that I have found to keep me organized and eliminate clutter and pretty much capture everything is called **Evernote**. https://evernote.com

This has been a game changer for me. It has taken most of the paper out of my life and eliminated the multiple tabs that I leave open in web browsers. This application works across platforms and is designed for note taking, organizing and archiving.

Evernote allows you to capture information from everywhere using whatever device you have at hand. Use it with your phone, Ipad, Computer. The application lets users create notes of photographs, scanned images, voice memos, webpages or web page excerpts. Then everything is searchable.

Outlook: To keep a calendar of upcoming book launches, events, freebie days and everything in between, I use Microsoft Outlook which now had an **Evernote** add-in. Office is personal information manager from Microsoft, available as a part of the Microsoft Office suite. I was introduced to Outlook through my former life in the 9-5.

Not only do I still use it for email, it also includes a calendar, task manager, contact manager, note taking, journal, and web browsing.

Lastly, you may want to invest in 'cloud storage' of some kind as a back-up to your work or simply when you want to transfer 'big' files in a secure environment. To meet this need I have only really used **Dropbox**. Which I already had to use from time to time in my other job. It can be found at www.Dropbox.com.

It comes with a with a single 9.99 fee per month, but will help you navigate hassles when it comes to super large files.

Chapter 4: The Business of Writing

I wanted to take a quick second to properly address the business end of writing. As an author, you are going to have a new revenue stream that you must give some thought to. You may want to even take it a step further and form a business entity. Talk with your accountant about it.

Whatever you spend in the course of 'writing' should be noted so that you can get the proper write-offs come tax time. I keep it simple and track everything I do with respect to expenses in excel.

As a writer, some of the more common expenses that you might incur are: website and hosting, cover creation, formatting & editing, word processing applications like Word and everything in between. All I am asking is that you keep an eye on things.

Amazon KDP and Amazon's Createspace will keep track of your earnings for you. Normally, you get paid 60 days after the sale (**Net 60**) of a book. The turnaround on the payment takes this long because of their return policy timelines. Also, when it comes time for pay Uncle Sam, Amazon has track of your earnings, so you merely have to take the reports from Amazon and your matching expense reports to your Accountant who will then hopefully find as many write-offs as possible.

Chapter 5: What is in a Typical Book?

I thought before I jumped into the mechanics of writing Erotica, that I would take a step back and give you're a general overview of just what constitutes a book.

In addition to the cover, what are the parts of a book? Whether the book is self-published or published in the traditional way, for the most part, books share a common structure and each element appears in a similar location in every book.

In general, there are 3 parts of a book:

1.   Front Matter

2.   Body Matter

3.   End Matter

What is a book's FRONT MATTER?

Front matter is the information that appears up front and first in a book. For example, some of the pieces front matter would include:

Title page – this is a page which contains the title of the book, the author (or authors) and the publisher. Copyright page — includes:

the declaration of copyright (that is, who owns the copyright, generally the authors)

other types of credits, such as illustrators, editorial staff, indexer, etc., and sometimes notes from the publishers

International Standard Book Number (**ISBN**)- ISBNs are the global standard for identifying titles **ISBNs** are used world-wide as a unique identifier for books. They are used to simplify distribution and purchase of books throughout the global supply chain.

Edition number — this number represents the number of the edition and of the printing.

Dedication — where the author honors an individual or individuals by declaring that the labor of the book is "To" [name or names]

Acknowledgements — the author's thanks to those who contributed time and resources towards the effort of writing the book.

Table of Contents — outlines what is in each chapter of the book.

Foreword — is a "set up" for the book, typically written by someone other than the author.

Preface — is a "set up" for the book's contents, generally by the author.

Introduction —introduces the material that is covered in the book. Here the author can set the stage for the reader, and prepare them for what can be expected from reading the book. The introduction is a way for the author to grab the reader's attention. In the introduction, the author can quickly and simply tell the reader what is to be revealed in much greater detail if they continue reading.

What is a book's BODY MATTER?

Body Matter is what is in the book. This content is most often divided into segments, most commonly chapters. If larger chunks are divided, they are called:

- Parts

- Sections

- Chapters

The body matter is numbered with Arabic numerals beginning with the number "1" on the first page of the first chapter.

What is a book's END MATTER?

End matter is the materials at the back of the book, generally optional.

Glossary — this is a listing and definitions of terms that might be unfamiliar to the reader.

Bibliography – most often seen in non-fiction like biography or in academic books, a bibliography lists the reference sources used in researching the book.

Index – An index is an optional but highly desirable element for non-fiction books. The index is placed at the end of the book and lists all the major references in the book (such as major topics, mentions of key people in the book, etc.) and their specific, corresponding page numbers. Note that even traditional publishers pass along the cost of hiring an indexer for the book to the author.

Together, **Front, Body and End Matter** are called 'Interior Matter' and they form to constitute your book.

Chapter 6: Some Writing Tips

Before I share tidbits like never use the words 'penis' or' vagina'. Let's take a step back and examine some basic writing tips. How do we approach this? How do we get started?

In practice, there are must know tips that will help you dive right in and get started.

Know your reader.

You should work out ahead of time who your reader and audience is going to be. Know your customer and product. You must know who your book is for and know that they will want to purchase it. Don't write a book for everyone. Write for a specific niche-- kink. For example, some niches to write on could be:

1. **Erotic Horror**

2. **Gay**

3. **Ménage**

4. **BDSM**

That aside, it has been demonstrated that the most successful authors are normally part of a group to whom they write about something. For example, if you were part of the punk rock music seen in NYC in the early eighties, you have a particular audience segment that would like to read about your experience. Perhaps you could have a Punk Ménage Book. Just food for thought.

Find a place, time and manner to write.

When, where and how will you write your book? These questions should be answered before you even sit down and write. Again, writing is work. It requires discipline. Personally, I have always preferred to work once everyone is asleep or first thing in the morning before everyone is awake. My spot of choice has always been the kitchen due to the lighting. When I write, I always aim to produce about 500- 1000 words in a sitting. In so doing, I ensure that the book keeps moving along. If you can do more, go for it.

Next, how are you going to write? These days, everyone seems to be using laptops, but that hasn't caught favor with me. My strong preference is still to write in longhand. Once you have a chapter of substance, you can simply type it into your word processing program. People like to tell me that this is inefficient. However, in this manner, you can literally do a first line edit on anything that you penned.

Plan and outline your book.

In a very real sense, this will help you set the boundaries of your book and keep you focused on the work at hand. At minimum, you should:

- Create a table of contents

- Write chapter summaries

- Evaluate the length of similar books published

- Determine the length you want

- Decide about how long each chapter will be

With this information you will have an excellent guide that will keep you on course and help you produce a book that is neither too short nor too long.

Quality matters.

Remember that quality matters. Not only should the book that you create have good ideas and a great story behind it, it should be presented with the least possible mistakes. Simply put, the book that you create is a reflection on you.   It has your name on it even if you choose to use a pen name or not it and you should do it right. Accordingly, you should have someone edit your book. In fact, the more rounds of editing that you can employ the better the book's outcome.

Chapter 7: A Word on Choosing your Topic

Now that the warm-up is over, we can jump right into the thick of things.

The first thing that you'll need to do is choose your topic. To do this, simply visit the Erotic Category on Amazon to see what is currently selling. To give you an idea of what is popular check the top 100 and the top 100 Not New Releases. Naturally, you want to pick a topic that you have some knowledge about.

Invariably, you are going to find that Taboo sells. Taboo includes various story types such as Pseudo-Incest, Multiple Partners, BDSM, Dubious Consent, Shapeshifters and everything in between

Pseudo-Incest: This is basically incest that isn't really incest. Be very careful with this subject, however. This would entail perhaps a stepbrother and stepsister story, or a stepfather and his stepdaughter.

Multiple Partners: Threesomes, ménage, group sex, etc. are always evergreen. People enjoy this category as it stands as one of the ultimate taboos. Men and women both fantasize about this kind of a thing. Please be sure to avoid the word 'gangbang' when writing about this sub-genre as Amazon will filter it.

BDSM: This involves capturing the practices involving bondage, dominance and submission, sadomasochism. Please do your homework on this topic, because this is a niche where the reader is very informed.

Dubious Consent: This involves anything related to reluctance, rape or near-rape. It has to appear non-consensual but be consensual. Therefore the 'victim' in this kind of thing must be someone such as a woman who somehow arranges to have her 'rape fantasy' acted out. In this way, the act now becomes consensual.

Shapeshifters: This audience was born from the Romance genre. I mean Disney has even touched on this subject with Beauty and The Beast. In order to pull this sub-genre off, I recommend writing at minimum an 8000 word story.

As you can see there is no shortage of topics to write about. Just be thorough about your study of each and ensure that you are comfortable with the subject matter that you write a story about. Needless to say, take your time develop you craft and be aware of its inherent nuances and caveats.

Chapter 8: The Erotic Story Structure – My Method

The reason you are writing in the first place is to embrace fantasy, right? You aren't writing about what you and your husband did last night before going to bed. You are writing to entertain fantasy and deep-seated desire. Erotic stories are written about the sexual journeys of the characters involved.

Although some may simply approach writing Erotica using a three-part structure that an entail just an **Introduction, Main Act (SEX)** and **Resolution**, the typical structure that I use is still built on what I learned all the way back in grammar school. It is just in this Genre the Climax is the Climax! These parts are: **Introduction, Twist/ Problem, Rising Tension, Sex, Climax and Resolution.**

1. Introduction (500 Words):

The Introduction contains all of the necessary background information that is needed to understand the story. In other words, it sets the stage. This information typically includes the characters, setting and circumstances.

The trick here is to humanize your main character in some way. They are like you and me. My main characters are almost always women. I make them powerful, but I give them anxieties, insecurities, frustrations. I introduce their past sexual history but tend to let their mind wander as to what they would want to do.

The men, I use them to my advantage. I mention their looks and appearance, if they are well dressed or casual. What is their demeanor? Are they strong and solid? Is there skin tanned? What is their hair color? What cologne are they wearing? You get the picture.

Same holds true if there are other women that crop up into the picture, I will describe their physicality. Do they have long legs? Is their skin glistening? Are they blonde, brunette? Are they tan? What perfume are they wearing?

2. Twist/ Problem (750 words):

The next part --The twist—is where I introduce you to some problem, obstacle or complication the main character is having. Perhaps, she is being blackmailed into having sex in order to move up the corporate ladder? Perhaps she was with her girlfriends out on the town and may have had a crush on one of her friends and she would like to explore this latent desire despite the fact that she views it as taboo. Maybe, she wants something that she can't have and must blackmail and manipulate to get what she wants. There is a myriad of options to choose from. Just pick one and go for it!

Just remember that the problem is something that is solved with sex.

3. Rising Tension – Obstacle That Will Be Overcome with Sex (1500-2500 words):

We then develop more of the story line built on this tension/ obstacle How are our characters are motivated what stands in the way. How do they overcome the obstacle?

Move your main character towards the solution—the sex. Build anticipation. There may be inner turmoil that is shooting through her mind that doesn't let her rest.

We are slowly building. Perhaps you have your main character who is bored to death with her husband and the unrest created is driving her to think of younger guys with chiseled bodies.

She knows that her husband has been good to her, but she is looking for more. Work on the build-up. Emotion and hesitation are good, but remember that these books are not romance novels, but erotica. The focus is still on the sex.

4. SEX (2000 Words):

Here is where they finally meet. Every moment is a build. Anticipation fills the scene. Build with foreplay to exploration to the main act. We want this to be off the charts. This is where sensual moves to graphic. The fireworks start here.

Again, if you are a first timer, study some other books just to see the nuances in how this is achieved. Take out your thesaurus. Show don't tell.

It is not the glistening forbidden fruit for nothing!

5. Climax (500-750 words):

Well we have finally made it. This is where all the build-up has brought us. This is where each of the participants reaches climax. This is where the story has reached its peak. It is the moment of greatest tension and relief. It is the orgasm.

The fireworks end here.

6. Resolution (300-500 words):

Here is where we wrap it up. These events are usually the after-effects of the climax. Here is where they recover from the exhausting sex. This is the kiss goodbye. This part ends the book or may leave off with room for more books down the road.

The dialog should suggest something like "we should meet up again". In that way, you could consider making a series of the book…

In any event, using this simple architecture has allowed me to develop stories more quickly and methodically than I had in the past. The word limits are suggestions. As a rule of thumb, for straight forward stories I use about 5000 words and for stories that need more development the aim is 8000 words.

25

Chapter 9: Publishing to Kindle – Make your eBooks

Congratulations! I am going to assume that you have finished your manuscript and have a completed book cover and you are ready to go. In this chapter, we are going to focus on how to get your book published on Kindle. To do so, you will have to set up your Kindle Direct Publishing Account (KDP) at http://kdp.amazon.com.

Once you are there, you will be prompted to provide your email address, assign a name to your account and establish a password. After this is complete, you'll need to acknowledge that you are in compliance with Amazon's Terms of Service by clicking the appropriate box. Please ensure that you do read these and don't simply check the box. You don't want to jeopardize your account one bit. If you were to violate any of their terms, you could possibly run the risk of having your account closed.

After this Acknowledgement, you will be prompted to set-up your account information. Here, you will need to provide your name or your company's name, address & telephone number.

Next, you will be prompted to provide a W-9 for tax reporting purposes. Simply, click on the Update Tax Information button and answer the brief tax interview that will generate a W-9 for KDP.

Once that is done, you will need to provide information with respect to how you would like to receive your royalty payments. You must specify if you want to receive your payment via check or by

Electronic Funds Transfer (EFT). Please note that if you do not set up a bank account and routing number, the default is to automatically send you a check at the address that you have previously provided.

Overview of KDP Dashboard

The KDP dashboard consists of only a few sections:

Bookshelf

The bookshelf is where you can view all of your books and publish new books.

Reports

In the reports section you can view your Month-To-Date Unit Sales, Prior Six Week's Royalties and Prior Month's Royalties.

Community

The community section consists of an online forum where you can interact with other Kindle publishers. This is very useful for asking any questions you have about publishing on Kindle and how everything works.

KDP Select

KDP Select is a program that you can enroll your books in that give you special advantages. People are able to "borrow" your books and you'll get paid for them, and you can also market your book for free for up to 5 days every 90 days. The downside is that your book (the ebook version) is exclusive only with Amazon and Kindle, so it can't be published anywhere else on the internet.

Uploading to Kindle

Before you start the upload process, you should gather all your information together in one place. Once the process is started, you should aim to get it done in one short process. However, if you need to discontinue your work you can break-off at any time and finish it up later. Just make sure to save it.

The Dashboard

Open your KDP screen and log in to your account. Choose Bookshelf and click on "Add New Title".

Book Name (required)

The first thing you will be prompted to enter is your Book Name. This should be the Title and Subtitle you have decided for your book, in exactly the way you would like it displayed on your Sales Page.

Series Number (optional)

Next, is your book part of a Series? Probably not if this is your first book, so ignore it. However, if it were in a series you would enter the series title here. Books with the same series title would automatically link and create a series landing page. Naturally, this will help your books in the series to get found by showing all the books in a series on a single page.

Edition Number (optional)

A version is a particular edition of your book. If this is the original, then enter the number 1. If you update your book with significant changes later on you can go back and enter the number 2.

Publisher (optional)

Enter the publisher that you would like listed for your e-book. This can be an individual or company name.

Description (required)

Next is Description. The book's description tells the readers something about your book and what it addresses. The description for your book is between 30 and 4000 characters.

Contributors (required)

Next comes the Book Contributors. The simple rule is not to give any credit away. If you wrote the book, and nobody else made a serious contribution, don't add anything here.

Language (required)

Enter the language of your book.

ISBN (optional)

If you have an International Standard Book Number (**ISBN**) for this e-book, you can use it here. Otherwise disregard, as Amazon doesn't require one and will assign a unique ASIN number to track it. If you already have a print version of your book, don't use it here.

Verifying Your Publishing Rights (required)

If the publishing rights to your work are privately held, please check "I hold the rights to this book". If it is a work of public domain, check the appropriate box for that.

Categories (required)

Next Choose your Categories. This will allow interested readers to find your book.

You can specify two, and you should. When you click on Add Categories you'll be presented with an exhaustive list of options. The best way to choose these initially is to look at your competitors and see which categories they are selling in.

Age and Grade Range (optional)

These are optional fields that make it easier to find your books. If you have, for example, an e-book that is designed for a second-grade level, enter the appropriate information here.

Enter Your Keywords (optional)

Next, you can enter up to seven keywords. Keywords are another very important element in your Marketing process, so pay attention to this and make them count. These keywords are considered as part of your book's metadata (the bunch of tags and details that are used by various search and ranking functions) and you will rank somewhere in every search that is made on these words.

Select Your Book Release Date (required)

You can either choose to make your book available for pre-order or make it available immediately. If you choose the pre-order option, you can start taking orders for your book 90 days in advance of its launch.

Upload your Cover

Next you will upload your book cover file. The cover is by far one of the most compelling pieces of a book. I strongly suggest that you have one made. No matter what they say, a book is judged by its cover!

Digital Rights Management (required)

As mentioned elsewhere, I'm not convinced that DRM has any significant effect for low-volume books. If you enable DRM, it should help to ensure that your book is protected against pirates who might steal it and make it available for sale or distribution on non-Amazon sites. There are a million reasons why this is a bad thing, so if you care about it, don't give them the opportunity.

Uploading your Book (required)

Next, you will upload your book file by Browsing and selecting the final file name. You can upload your original .doc or .docx manuscript document and KDP will reformat it accordingly. Alternately, you can upload an HTML file, which is really only useful if you have included some advanced HTML formatting. These options are explored in the next section. Shortly afterwards you will see the KDP system performing the Conversion and it should return a Green Tick to tell you that the conversion has been successful. It will also spell check your manuscript and tell you if it finds errors. If there are mistakes you will be given the opportunity to inspect the file, and you'll need to make corrections.

Online Kindle Previewer

Now you can view your book in the Online Previewer, which you should do. This version allows you to see all the different Kindle devices as well as the Apple iPhone and iPad, which is really useful. Go through each device and look at as many pages as you can find time for. If you see any serious formatting issues at this stage, you'll need to fix them in your original manuscript, and repeat the upload process with a new version of your file. Once you are satisfied, click back to your Book Information in the top right corner.

You now have a choice of Save as a Draft, which allows you to move onto the next stage without committing the information or Save and Continue which will upload all the information you entered to Amazon and start the formatting and approval process ready to construct your book's Sales Page.

 If you select Save as Draft you can come back shortly and change things if you wish, but you cannot proceed to the next stage until you click on Save and Continue.

Territories and Publishing Rights (required)

The Second Page starts with Section 8 where you select your publishing Territories. Unless you have a specific reason not to do so, choose Worldwide Rights, which will ensure that your book goes up on all Amazon websites all around the globe for maximum exposure. On the other hand, should you not take this option, you can choose piecemeal from roughly 245 territories.

Pricing and Royalty (required)

There are two royalty schemes:

35%, or

70%

To get a royalty on you book of 70% you must price it between 2.99 USD to 9.99 USD. Otherwise you will get 35% for pricing your book from .99 USD to 2.98 USD and anything from 10.00 USD to 200.00 USD. Naturally, we want to select the 70% royalty.

Kindle Matchbook (optional)

Click the box if you want to enroll in the Kindle Matchbook program. The Kindle matchbook program gives customers who have previously purchased your print book from Amazon the option to purchase your Kindle version for 2.99 USD or less if you have a print version of your title and roll your title and select the promotional list price that is lower than your Kindle list price by at least 50%.

Kindle Book Lending (optional)

Section 10 is to enable Kindle Book Lending, which allows Kindle owners to lend the book to their friends or family. Click the box and allow lending.

Save and Publish (required)

That's it. All you need to do now is tick the disclaimer box below to confirm you agree the Terms and Conditions. If you are ready to go, click Save and Publish. You'll receive an e-mail from Amazon once your book is live on the site. The Kindle Store requires approximately 12 hours to update titles.

Chapter 10: Publishing to CreateSpace - Make a Paperback

Why not take it a step further and create a printed version of your e-book? You can easily accomplish this by using CreateSpace which is Amazon's print on demand (POD) Service. Getting a book printed in this manner, ensures that production runs don't require an initial cash outlay from the author/ publisher. Essentially, a book is printed as ordered by the customer.

The process is very similar to the one used in the previous chapter. In order to upload your formatted manuscript to CreateSpace you are going to need to create an account at www.createspace.com. You should use the same email address you used for your Kindle book as it will facilitate the marriage of each of the hardcopy and e-book version of your book on Amazon.com.

Start a New Project:

From your membership dashboard click on the blue **add new title button**. This will take you to the **Start your New Project** page. Fill in the name of the book and select 'Paperback' as the Type of Project and then choose the Guided Set-up Method

 By clicking **Get Started**, this will bring you to the next step.

Title Information:

On this page, provide the book title, sub-title (if applicable), author name, contributors, series name & number (if applicable and other details. If your work is non-fiction be sure to include important keywords in the title and sub-title. Moreover, if you have published previously to Kindle use the publication of the e-book version in the Publication Date area. This will further facilitate the marriage of each of the versions by Amazon. Then, click Save& Continue.

ISBN:

Next, you will be asked to choose an ISBN option for your book. An ISBN (number) is required to publish and distribute a book. There are four choices that you can elect from.

Do your homework as to your best option. My favorite is the first version as it is free, but it carries the CreateSpace Independent Publishing Platform Imprint. If you plan, to use Amazon as your principle source of distribution this, in my opinion, is the best route. Do, however, choose your option carefully as it can't be changed once you have set it.

ISBN stands for International Standard Book Number. Each ISBN is a unique numerical identification code and all books published since 1965 have had an ISBN. If you publish your book in different formats, for example paperback, hardcover, or e-book, each variation needs a different ISBN. You will remember, however, in the Kindle publishing process that an ISBN is completely optional, and Kindle does not assign ISBN's for E-books. When your book is printed, the ISBN is also translated into a barcode by CreateSpace. This satisfies the key functions of the ISBN, which is firstly to enable bookshops and distribution channels to identify your book for ordering purposes, and secondly the barcode enables them to manage it within their P.O.S and stock system. Once you've made a note of your ISBN, click Continue.

Interior:

Next, you'll have to choose what your pages are going to look like. You can choose between black & white or color. Then, you'll need to choose a paper color. You can select between cream or white paper.

Trim size:

Then, you are going to have to select a trim size. Although you can select a custom size, please do yourself a favor and pick an industry standard size as this will allow you to sell your book through Expanded Distribution Channels.

Books with cream paper must be one of the following trim sizes: 5 x 8 inches, 5.25 x8 inches, 5.5 x 8.5 inches or, 6 x 9 inches in order to enroll in the Expanded Distribution Channels.

Industry standard for books that are black & white are: 5 x 8 inches, 5.06 x 7.81 inches, 5.25 x 8 inches, 5.5 x 8.5 inches, 6 x 9 inches, 6.14 x 9.21 inches, 6.69 x 9.61 inches, 7 x 10 inches, 7.44 x 9.69 inches, 7.5 x 9.25 inches, 8 x 10 inches, 8.25 x 6 inches, 8.25 x 8.25 inches, 8.5 x 8.5 inches and 8.5 x 11m inches.

Margins:

Gutter margins are by the book's binding. You'll want a wider margin for longer (thicker) books. See the table for what to set your inside margins to.

Outside margins are the page edges opposite of the binding, and the top and bottom margins. All live text and images must have an outside margin of at least .25" -- but we recommend an outside margin of at least .5"

Please adhere to the following:

Page Count	Inside Margin	Outside Margins
24 to 150 pages	.375"	at least .25"
151 to 300 pages	.5"	at least .25"
301 to 500 pages	.625"	at least .25"
501 to 700 pages	.75"	at least .25"
701 to 828 pages	.875"	at least .25"

With respect to Trim Size, take a trip to your local bookstore and choose a size relative to your genre. If you have a lot of pictures, however, you may want to choose a larger trim size for display purposes. Also, try to ensure that you have at minimum 120 pages for your book, so that when it comes time to add on a cover there is enough room for a proper spine so that you can add the title to the spine. A book tends to get lost on the shelf if it doesn't have a proper title down the spine.

Formatting with Templates

OK, once you have settled on a book size you can select a template. Download a Microsoft Word Template, either a blank template or a formatted template with sample content designed for the trim size you choose.   I use 6 x 9 inches as they recommend it.

If you are publishing for the first time and the formatting is straightforward, the formatted template is a very useful. It sets up Chapter Headers, Page Numbers, and Page Headers, as well as showing you where to insert all your front material such as **Title** and **Author Name**, **Copyright Information**, **Dedications** and **Contents**.

However, if your book has more complicated and contains things like Subheadings, Section Titles, Numbered Lists, Bullet Points, Indents, Diagrams or Pictures, then please don't use the formatted template. Instead, the blank template, which simply sets up the Word document with margins. In the case of both these templates, the gutter offsets (for left and right-hand pages) are perfectly setup to ensure that your printed book will look professional. With the non-formatted template, you are free to choose your own standard CreateSpace recognized fonts and type size.

Upload your work as a print-ready **.pdf, .doc, .docx**, or **.rtf** file.

After you upload your formatted manuscript and it goes through the Createspace automated print check, view your book page by page using the Interior Reviewer.

If CreateSpace catches formatting errors, you will need to fix them and re-upload. Naturally, this can be a bit time consuming, but it is par for the course. In the event, you can't figure out the glitch, email or call CreateSpace Support. Their people helped me through a couple roadblocks when I set up my first book.

Cover:

Choose a finish for your book cover, either matte or glossy.

Next, choose how to submit your book cover. There are three methods:

- Build Your Cover Online with Cover Creator, a free Createspace tool to design your book covers.

- Professional Cover Design by CreateSpace, starting at $399.

- Upload a Print-Ready PDF Cover: Createspace provides detailed instructions for this method.

No matter what they say, people will judge a book by its cover. Therefore, my strong advice is to get professional help and enlist a design service. Google the words '**cover design**' and see what you find. Once you have a suitable cover, with a front, spine & back done to the correct standards, then and only then, can you upload.

Complete Setup:

Review your project setup. If everything looks okay, submit your files for review. You can go back and make changes if you need to. When ready, submit for review.

Review:

The CreateSpace automated review program makes sure your work passes muster for "manufacturing and cataloging".

Proof your book:

If it does, you will be asked if you want to order a proof copy (at cost) for your final approval. I always do this because there could still be issues that need correcting.

Distribution Channels:

Choose your distribution channels and choose **Expanded Distribution**.

Pricing:

Set a price for your book. Use the built-in calculator to determine what the royalties will be. Keep in mind that distributors usually discount the book price and Amazon will match the discounted price. If you set your price too low, your proceeds will suffer when the book is discounted. Of course, you don't want to price your book so high that it scares off readers.

Description:

Provide a description for your sales page. Assign a BISAC Category; add your author bio; set language, country of publication; choose search keywords; check for adult content if applicable and if you want large print.

Final approval:

When you are satisfied, give Createspace the go-ahead to publish your print book. When you're absolutely certain that your book is the way you wanted it to look, you can then approve your proof by clicking on the approve button.

Publish on Kindle:

If you have chosen to do your CreateSpace Print on Demand project before you have you Kindle version, it is possible to automatically publish an identical version to Kindle. This screen will appear automatically, and if you would like to do this please do take advantage by clicking on the big blue button.

Once your book is live, CreateSpace will alert you.

Chapter 11: Get a Sexy Cover & Get the Pricing Right!

<u>Your Cover</u>

The most important part of the book is arguably your cover.

Although we don't like to admit it, a book is judged by its cover! In essence, your cover can make or break you. Your cover can have a direct impact on the reader's purchasing decisions and adding a high-quality cover image is an effective way for you to inspire customer confidence and boost sales.

Investigate what covers look like in Erotica and ensure that your cover can stand with the best of them. If you are unsure go directly to www.fiverr.com . Most are Amazon compliant and will be able to guide you along.

<u>Get the Pricing Right</u>

As stated previously, if you are enrolled in Kindle Select you are obligated to price between 2.99 USD to 9.99 USD. To be eligible for the discount deals or free promotions and the 70% royalty. Take inventory of your competition. See what the going rate is and try to undercut them if possible. If your competition is at 4.99 USD try 3.99 to employ a market penetration strategy. If your book is a specialty book and you are in Kindle Select you might want to price it at 9.99USD to engage in a Skimming strategy.

If you have multiple books out, the 0.99 USD price point has come strongly into favor. That said, this is probably the best penetration strategy and will sell the most copies once you have been established. However, this precludes you from Kindle Select and will only garner you a 35% royalty rate.

Chapter 12: Get your Website

If you see traction for your book(s), you might want to consider a website. Again, up to you.

When I was new to the idea of getting a website together, I basically panicked until I came across the company 1&1 http://www.1and1.com/ the provided a fast and easy means to create a hosted website with no prior knowledge of HTML and stuff like that. The package is called MyWebsite. I was on a learning curve but I enjoyed it.

It freed me from the shackles of a webmaster who was my friend, but completely ineffective and non-responsive despite the friendship. He thought he was saving me money, but he was costing me instead.

I have become better versed in a whole host of applications that I use operate my business. Now, I have been toying with some new word press themes and have moved in the direction of Joanna Penn who has a brilliant tutorial on her site if you want to go this route: **http://www.thecreativepenn.com/2015/08/13/build-author-website/.**

Your website, in addition to being your online business card is your store and relationship builder. Remember, to use it to build your list and community. You may want to go a bit further and use email sign-up widgets on your website. The old trick is to offer a sample chapter of your upcoming book in exchange for an email. Visit a www.mailchimp.com or try www.aweber.com.

Lastly, if you will use images of yourself on your website, make sure that is done by a professional, as it will be your avatar in cyberspace.

41

Chapter 13: Create an Author Central Profile

If you're selling books on Amazon, you should set up your page in their Author Central to introduce yourself to your readers.

Creating a compelling author page takes just a few minutes and will help readers learn more about you and your books as they shop Amazon's site. Ensure your author profile is complete. You can use Author Central to upload your picture, add a biography, view and edit your bibliography, and create a blog to speak directly to readers.

To set up you Amazon Author Central page, go to: http://authorcentral.com.

Again, as on your website, if your use pictures of yourself here make sure they are professional. As an author it pays itself back in spades to have a professional photographer take your headshots and pictures. Like in the case of the book cover, people actually judge you on your photograph. Think of it as your Avatar that lives in cyberspace that has a life of its own.

Sometimes people would like to shortcut this critical element as redundant and as an unnecessary expense. However, we should be actually looking at it an opportunity to capture who we are and show the face behind the book or business.

In short, the shot must be able to convey your personal brand.

In addition to establishing your presence as an author, this has the added value of humanizing you for your reader. Also, having an author profile gives you the opportunity to cross-promote your books, since when people click on your profile, they will then see all of the other books that you've published under that profile. Just think of this as free publicity.

43

Chapter 14: A Word on Pen Names:

When writing books for the Erotica / Romance genre it is quite typical to use pen names. This is done for a variety of reasons. Perhaps you want to keep your real name confidential? Perhaps you want to multiply the reach of your books across different pen names in order to make more money? Last, I checked, per account, Amazon allows 3 different author names. Perhaps you just want a cooler sounding name than your god given name?

Whatever the case, writers have been using pen names forever. In fact, Mark Twain was a pen name.

For starters, you should probably pick an easy name that is catchy. All of your initial work should probably be done under this name as you learn the ropes.

Once you get going and are quite comfortable, you'll then want to pick a pen name to assign per kink/theme within the Erotica umbrella. For example, something as obvious as Mistress Anne may work for BDSM.

Just remember that until you are ready to branch out like that, just pick a name that is simple, yet disposable to learn with.

Chapter 15: Choose your Keywords Wisely:

It may not be natural to associate Amazon which is an online retailer as a search engine, but in the technology sector, you never know where your next competitive threat can come from.

That said, the ecommerce search engine optimization (SEO) community seems to be missing a window of opportunity by focusing their marketing efforts primarily on Google, while they should be focusing in on Amazon because it roughly has three times more search volume for product searches. Just two years ago, Google's main competition would have been Yahoo and Bing, but today at least in the product search space Amazon trumps its competition.

While we were all busy Googling, Amazon has moved into becoming the leading product search engine and this is presently where it stands. Similar to ranking on the first page of Google with website content, ranking well in the Amazon's Kindle Store allows your content to get discovered long after you put in initial marketing effort. That's why optimizing for keyword and category ranking is key.

Therefore, from a business perspective, a book on Amazon about your discipline would increase traction for your business and open up the chance to consider other alternatives to Google. Accordingly, spending more time optimizing on Amazon translates into better awareness and sales for you.

For keywords and categories, your ranking is determined by

- Number of positive reviews

- Total downloads

- Total revenue

In addition to this, do keep in mind that your book title and metadata are important for keywords.

You Should Remember:

The primary way that customers search on Amazon is by keywords that are matched against search terms for their product. Well-chosen search terms will increase a product's visibility and sales. Moreover, price, reviews & sales history are taken into consideration relative to where the product will rank.

Chapter 16: Get Social

Social Media is defined as an online site or platform that connects people who share similar interests. These sites are invaluable marketing tools when used effectively because they allow people and businesses to share events, activities and ideas within a network that they build. As of April 2012, social networking accounted for 22% of all time spent online. Translation: your customers are using social media a lot; you should too.

So why should you invest your time building out a social media presence? The answer is a no-brainer: using social media allows you to reach your clients and customers faster and more inexpensively that ever before. You are fostering a community interested in you and your book and allowing them to have the latest information about you and your book.

Some of the most common social media sites are:

- Facebook

- Twitter

- LinkedIn

All, for the most part, allow individuals and businesses to stay connected with their potential customers. While the various platforms are similar in their use, each has its own set of nuances that you can take advantage of to make connections with your prospective client base.

In the main, all of these social media platforms adhere to the same formula: users connect with others and encourage friends, followers and colleagues to connect back with them.   You can post information about your book on your sites that then will be shared with friends, colleagues and followers. Remember as a writer, the goal isn't to have the most followers, but to have a targeted group interested in you and your book.

Facebook:

By far the world's largest social media platform with close to a billion users, can be used to connect you with customers for your book. You can have a personal page and one for your book. Use Facebook to make an author page if you want to present more information about you and your book.

Twitter:

Twitter is a "micro-blogging" platform where all communication takes place in 140-character "tweets" or posts. Twitter users broadcast over 40 million tweets each day . You can link to blog posts, images and more within your tweets. Use Twitter, if you prefer more informal conversation to reach your target audience.

LinkedIn:

Very similar to Facebook, but with a business bent, LinkedIn can be used for professional networking. It allows you to connect with people within your field and allows you to show your business activity.

Every social media site has its set of advantages and disadvantages. Used consistently and effectively they can be a very inexpensive way to reach your target audience. By keeping you book 'branding' initiative in mind, your social media presence will work to reinforce getting the word out across the internet.

Your List:

Make sure that when you have something to announce let your following know immediately via the list that you have generated with your website. If you have a new book put, let them know.

Chapter 17: YouTube & Vimeo Videos

Like Google and like Amazon, YouTube and Vimeo are popular search engines, but are geared towards videos. Every day, there are millions of people doing searches for material on them. If you were to create a trailer video for your book and optimize it for keywords, just as you did for Amazon or Google for that matter, this could reach more of your target market. What's more, you could then take that video and place it on your Amazon Author Central page and on your website, which would have a link to the Amazon book which would then aid in your overall SEO strategy.

Let's say you had a Kindle Book on cooking, you could then make a couple of videos and put them on YouTube. You could possibly do a quick cooking demonstration of a recipe in the book, upload it to YouTube optimizing it for keywords. In this video you could then add a link to your book and say: "For this recipe and many more, check out my book on Kindle."

This method with the call to action at the end is actionable advice that truly delivers. This simple video could help to drive more sales and reach more of your target. If you don't have the equipment to produce a video or are just camera shy, you can easily get a video done on fiverr.com for your book.

Chapter 18: KDP SELECT Free Promotion & Kindle Countdown Deals

When you list a book on Kindle, Amazon typically starts marketing the book for you right away.

Places where Amazon markets your book to customers on the Amazon website may include:

- More Items to Consider

- Customers with Similar Searches Purchased

- Customers Who Bought This Item Also Bought

Your book may also appear in Shopping Cart Recommendations, "Frequently Bought Together," and many other places on the Amazon website.

KDP Select Free Promotion

However, Amazon offers a free promotion feature though KDP Select that you can enroll in when you set up your book. Basically, KDP allows you to promote your book for up to five days for free every 90 days. This helps you to get more exposure by getting more downloads of your KDP e-book. Not only will it help with exposure, it will help to boost your keyword rankings and book rankings as well.

Here are some few tips for running your KDP Select Free Promotion:

- If you can try to break up your 5 days in to two pieces for the beginning of two separate weeks. That is, you could run a free book promotion for Monday & Tuesday of week 1 and perhaps Sunday, Monday & Tuesday of week two. The data suggests that the beginning of the week is the best time for the free promotions. Alternatively, if you don't have the time to break it up into two pieces, you could use all your days in one long stretch. In other words, you could set your free period from Sunday to Thursday.

- No matter how you choose to allocate your days, please ensure that you are promoting it in the background and through varied marketing channels. Make sure to use social media and also to let various book groups know that your book will be free during these days. Your aim is to have as many downloads as possible so that the book is perched for success in the rankings.

- Lastly, you will see a bump in sales when the free period ends. Do price your book between 2.99 – 9.99 USD to ensure that you get the 70 Percent royalty rate.

<u>Add a Kindle Countdown Deal Promotion.</u>

List your book in a limited-time KDP Select discount promotion that incrementally raises prices as time passes. This should be used once your book is established. When customers visit your book's page, they'll see the discount, and how long they have to buy before the price goes up. You'll set the discounts and the time periods. Promotions start at the lowest price, and over time, the price goes up to the next promotional list price, until the promotion completes and the original list price is restored. This is available for a 5 day time period. During each promotional day, your book's detail page will display a counter announcing the promotion, the current price, the time remaining until the price changes, and the next price.

Furthermore, Amazon will promote your book during this time on its dedicated Kindle Countdown Deals website and will allow you to take 70% of your royalties during this promotional period although the pricing can be beneath the $2.99 threshold. Naturally, the method should be used after you have used your free promotion and the book is established and has traction.

53

Chapter 19: Promoting on E-Book Websites, Facebook Groups, Forums & Twitter

In conjunction with your KDP Select Free days or discount days you should do everything in your capacity to get the word out through various websites, Facebook groups, forums and Twitter.

Remember you are trying to optimize your downloads for your Kindle e-book to raise its ranking and increase its sales traction once this free period or discount is lifted.

Below please find a listing of these websites, Facebook groups and Forums. Some of these are:

Websites:

http://awesomegang.com/submit-your-book/

http://authormarketingclub.com/members/announce-your-free-book/

 http://ebookspice.com/submissions

http://www.eroticaeveryday.com/

Facebook:

Facebook pages to post to on the days of promotion -

Please don't spam in these groups.

https://www.facebook.com/booksdirect

http://www.facebook.com/groups/authorspostyourbooks/

http://www.facebook.com/ebooksfreefreefree

https://www.facebook.com/groups/3698675030682261/

https://www.facebook.com/eReaderLove

http://www.facebook.com/readingkindle

http://www.facebook.com/IndieKindleWLC

http://www.facebook.com/pages/Kindle-Finds/217115528350246

http://www.facebook.com/iauthor

http://www.facebook.com/eReader1.US

https://www.facebook.com/pages/Share-FREE-eBooks/146399952110055

https://www.facebook.com/groups/FreeTodayOnAmazon/

http://www.facebook.com/AmbitiousBookClub

http://www.facebook.com/authormarketingclub . http://www.facebook.com/eReaderPerks

http://www.facebook.com/FreeDigitalReads

https://www.facebook.com/Ebookdealoftheday

http://www.facebook.com/pages/Free-Books-for-Kindle-UK/246923732000349?ref=ts&fref=ts

http://www.facebook.com/FreeKindleUK?ref=ts&fref=ts

http://www.facebook.com/pages/Free-for-Kindle-UK/217334871681796?ref=ts&fref=ts

http://www.facebook.com/Ireadon?ref=ts&fref=ts

http://www.facebook.com/pages/UK-Kindle-Book-Lovers/175617412524192?ref=ts&fref=ts

http://www.facebook.com/getfreeebooks?ref=ts&fref=ts

http://www.facebook.com/fkbooks?ref=ts&fref=ts

http://www.facebook.com/freeebookdeal?ref=sgm

https://www.facebook.com/groups/freetoday/

http://www.facebook.com/FreeBookClub.org

http://www.facebook.com/christianbookreaders

Forums:

Forums that you can post to on the day.

These forums allow you to sign up and post one thread about your book to them.

http://www.mobileread.com/forums/forumdisplay.php?f=226

http://www.kindleboards.com/index.php/board,42.0.html

http://www.worldliterarycafe.com/forum/171

Twitter:

On the day of your free promotion you can also piggyback on Twitter. For more traction, tweet to some of the following Twitter handles:

@ibdbookoftheday   @Booksontheknob   @kindle_free @freeebooksdaily

@kindlefreebooks @freedailybooks @free2kindle @freereadfeed @digitalinktoday

@fkbt @kindlestuff @free_kindle_fic @ebook @freeebookdeal @free @free_kindle

@freebookdude   @4FreeKindleBook   @FreeKindleStuff @IndAuthorSucess

@kindleebooks   @KindleBookKing   @KindleFreeBook
@KindleUpdates @Kindle_promo

@KindleDaily

So, to wrap this chapter up, just remember to use some of the strategies outlined above to increase your downloads and therefore your ranking on Amazon. Just remember that, at the minimum, listing on the **Facebook groups** and the **FREE websites** is a must for your book to be successful during the free days of discount days.

Chapter 20: Get Reviews

If you were looking for a great Thai restaurant, I am almost certain that you would check out the reviews on Thai Restaurants in your area before booking a reservation. Similarly, if you were looking to purchase a book, I am certain that you would look at the reviews before your final purchase. The bottom line is that reviews matter.

Reviews play a significant role in the ranking and the sales of your book. Consider them virtual word-of mouth. After all, books that get favorable reviews are those that appeal to the reader.   Many times, just seeing great reviews on a book is enough for someone to make that final click and purchase your book. For authors, good reviews are the catalysts that drive great sales!

How do we get those reviews?

Before we get started on strategies to help you get book reviews, I wanted to take a step back and ensure that you are in compliance with Amazon's Terms of Service in acquiring them. Bear in mind that Amazon expressly forbids:

"Reviews written for any form of compensation other than a free copy of the product. This includes reviews that are part of any paid publicity package."

I wanted to mention this very quickly because there are a host of websites and servicers that will for a fee post reviews about your book. These are off limits. Don't waste your time or money on them, as you could jeopardize your relationship with Amazon.

That aside, let's get started on getting ethical reviews for your book.

1. **Get the word out about your book.**

Tell your family, friends, neighbors and colleagues about your book. Post it on Facebook, tell people about it on LinkedIn. Wherever there is a crowd on social media, get the word out. Don't be afraid to ask their honest opinion on it. In this manner, you can get your book in front of hundreds of people who may give you a review.

2. **Review other people's books.**

Another strategy that is with Amazon's Terms of Service are to write reviews for other people. How is this going to help you? Short answer: there are other people in your shoes that are looking for reviews as well. The trick is to find someone who is in the free promotional stages with their book that don't have reviews yet. You can readily find these in free promotional groups within Facebook that I mention in chapter 14. Simply, write an honest review of their work and see if they will post a review for a free promotional book in return.

3. **Join the KDP Select Program.**

Lastly and most importantly, the former strategies should coincide with joining the KDP Select Program which allows you to promote your book for 5 days every 90 days. Naturally, this can help you get a lot of downloads. This can mean getting your book in front of hundreds, if not thousands of people. The probability is good that a few of them will go back and write a review. What's more, to help your prospects that a reader will ultimately leave a review, you should put a simple Call to Action in the Conclusion of you book. That states the following: **If you found this book to be of value, please take a moment to write a review on Amazon. Thank you for your time.**

Don't underestimate the power of the "review" in your overall success of your book marketing campaign on Amazon. It's one of the major keys to your book's success. Keep an eye on it and you will do just fine.

Chapter 21: Your Writing Challenge

As I get ready to end this book I am going to leave you with a story concept that you can develop on you own.

Using the tools and knowledge that I covered in this book I would like for you to write your own story from this premise.

<u>The story's rough premise:</u>

What I would like for the main character is a powerful corporate woman (say a CEO based out of LA) who is having trouble with relationship struggles who travels to Montreal for meetings. She could perhaps work in fashion or something else and be in Montreal up there looking for trends. The main thing is that I want it to be a kind of a reverse of Fifty Shades.

Once she gets there, after her rough flight, at the hotel she hires a masseuse and then...

The concept is something that you can run with. It can be very steamy, or you can go lighter on the erotica. Remember, either will be acceptable for Amazon publishing so it is up to you there.

The length depends on what you want from the story.

If you want the focus to be the session with the masseuse, then 4500-5000 words should be plenty to set up who she is, the scene, and the wrap up the story.

If you want to add a little more seduction time you could move towards 8000 words. For example, she informs him of what kinky thing she wants, and he is unsure, so he declines the session. Of course, she's a powerful business woman, so his boss is going to pressure him to apologize to her. She is understanding of the situation, but it gives her the chance to talk to him and find out why he was reluctant. After they talk, he is willing to go.

You could even take it further and go with a 10000-word count. Perhaps you want to switch between both character's Point of View and include some other sub plot, maybe some high-power situation that she is trying to unwind from.

Take the story and run with it. Maybe it will be good enough to publish!

Happy Writing!

GLOSSARY

A

Acid-Free Paper: Acid-free paper is paper that contains little or no acid to prevent it from yellowing from age.

Acknowledgments Page: The acknowledgments page is where the author recognizes those who morally supported the author or helped the author in the process of writing the book. It is typically found after the copyright page, but sometimes appears at the end of the book.

Acquisitions Editor: The acquisitions editor is the first editor to consider a book for publication at a traditional publishing house.

Addendum: The addendum is supplemental material found near the beginning of the book to site corrections or changes made to the text. It is generally used when correcting the text would disrupt the schedule or production process.

Advance Copies: Advance copies are books shipped by the printer to the publisher in advance of the shipping date of the main print run. They are often used for reviews and testimonials.

Annotate (Annotation): Annotation is a specific comment made to clarify a portion of the text. Annotations are normally placed somewhere in the page margins.

Appendix (Appendices): An appendix is a list of additional information, such as resources, that are not appropriate to list within the main body of the text.

Aqueous Coating: Aqueous coating is a water-based clear coating on a book's cover that enhances the colors while providing protection from fingerprints, stains, smudges, and scratches.

Art Paper: Art paper is a quality smooth coated paper (stock) best used for printing books that require quality reproduction of photographs, artwork and other images.

ASIN: The Amazon Standard Identification Number (ASIN) is a 10-character alphanumeric unique identifier assigned by Amazon.com and its partners for product identification within the Amazon.com organization.

Author's Copies: Author's copies are complimentary books given to an author as part of their publishing contract. providing ten free copies is typical, but more copies may be negotiated. This doesn't happen on CreateSpace.

Author Corrections: Author corrections are the changes made by an author to the text at the proofing stage.

Autobiography: An autobiography is a book a person writes about his or her life story.

B

 Backlist Titles: Backlist titles are books that have been published about six months earlier. The backlist, which is usually found less predominantly in a publisher's catalog or online, is the lifeblood of most successful publishing companies.

Back Matter: Back matter is additional information, such as the appendix, bibliography, index, notes, and other references. Back matter typically appears after the last chapter of the book but occasionally at the end of each chapter.

Back Orders: Back orders are the accumulation of all book pre-sales prior to printing.

Back-of-the-Room Sales: Back-of-the-room sales are direct-to-consumer non-bookstore sales made at special events where the author is the host, speaker, or a guest.

Barcode: A barcode is comprised of lines of varying widths contained in a small box. Barcodes are typically found on the back covers of books (and on many other products). An optical scanner reads the lines to identify the product's retail price, while also managing inventory for that title.

Bibliography: A bibliography is a listing of research resources and other materials used in the process of writing a book. Bibliographic references are often made in the text throughout the book.

BISAC: (Book Industry Standards and Communications) codes are a "standard used by many companies throughout the supply chain to categorize books based on topical content."

Binding: Binding is the method used to hold the book's signatures (pages) together. Examples are saddle stitch, wire-o, perfect bound, and casebound.

Biography: A biography is a book written about part or all of another person's life.

BLAD (Book Layout and Design): A BLAD is a brochure about a forthcoming book used to generate advance sales and media interest. The BLAD, typically 4 to 8 pages, displays the cover, a sample of the interior design, and a description of the book and author. It also includes the book's size and page number specifications, publication date, and contact and ordering information.

Bleeds (Bleeding or Bleed): Bleeds are an extension of color or another design element that extends beyond the crop marks and off the edge of the paper. Bleeds are trimmed after printing to give the effect of printing on colored paper or to maximize the visual impact and aesthetics of the design.

Blind Embossing (blind emboss): Blind embossing is the process of embossing without the use of ink or foils. The embossing is the same color as the paper being embossed and provides a subtle, classy, three-dimensional effect.

Bluelines: Bluelines are an inexpensive set of paper proof made from the negative films, showing all the colors in blue. They are used to check for typos and other errors and glitches where color is not a factor.

Blurb: A blurb is a brief, compelling quote from an author or reviewer about a book found on the back cover.

Boards: Boards are the heavy stock that the casewrap is glued to in the making of a hardcover book.

Boiler Plate: A boiler plate is also referred to as a template from which a publishing contract is negotiated. It is also sometimes referred to as the basic design template from which a book is designed.

Book Block: The book block is the book after is has been printed, gathered, and trimmed but not yet bound.

Book Club: Aside from the social meaning, a book club is a retail bookseller usually online or mail order that offers a selection of discounted popular books by category. Publishers sell quantities of books to book clubs at very deep discounts. In some cases, a book club purchases the rights to print a book in a special format.

Book Page: A book page a web page that contains information about a book and its author. It may include the book's cover, a summary of the book, an excerpt, purchasing information, an author bio and photo, a video trailer for the book, a blog link, and purchasing information.

Bookplate: A bookplate is a decorative sticker glued to the inside cover of a book that contains a line for the author's signature. Some publishers print and ship bookplates to authors to sign them. The quantity is then shipped back to the publisher, and on to the factory, where a machine affixes the bookplate at a location inside the book as specified by the publisher. Bookplates also may be used to identify numbered limited editions.

Book Signing: A book signing is an event, usually held at a bookstore, where the author of a book is set up at a table to autograph his or her book for customers. Book signings also occur at trade shows, speaking engagements, and other events where the author is the featured guest.

Book Trade: Book trade is referred to as the retail book market. It is used in distribution contracts to distinguish which sales types are exclusive to the distributor and which remain with the publisher. The book trade may consist of retailers such as Amazon and Barnes & Noble. Examples of sales excluded from the book trade are special sales, such as book clubs and mail order.

Book Trailer: A book trailer is a video about a book and its author, usually with the author as the host. A book trailer also may be recorded in an interview fashion or completely without the author present.

Bulk: The bulk is actual thickness of the paper used in producing a book. How the paper bulks is the thickness of the book once it has been printed and bound. It helps the publisher determine its perceived value. It also helps the book designer to know the width of the spine for copy placement.

C

Camera-Ready Copy: Camera-ready copy is the final layout of the book and/or cover.

Caption: A caption is a line of text that describes an accompanying photograph, chart, or illustration.

Casebound: A casebound book is a hardcover book with a paper or cloth casewrap glued to its boards. It typically also has head and tail bands.

Casewrap: Casewrap is paper or cloth that is glued to the boards of a book, thus making it casebound (hardcover).

Character Count (Characters): The character count is the total number of letters, spaces, numbers, and punctuation contained in a sentence, paragraph, or manuscript.

CIP (Cataloging in Publication): A CIP is a block of descriptive information, typeset in a specific format, that is found on the copyright page of a book. The CIP is used by libraries to catalog books for reference purposes.

CMYK: CMYK represents cyan, magenta, yellow, and key (black); the four process colors used to print a full-color image.

Coated Paper: Coated paper is a smooth, clay-coated paper used to print books when reproducing high-quality photographs and illustrations is important.

Co-Edition (Co-Publishing): A co-edition is the simultaneous publishing of the same book by two publishers for different markets. In most cases, co-editions involve publishers from two different countries.

Collate (Collated): Collating means organizing pages-and accounting for them-in the proper order.

Color Balance: The color balance is the proper intensity of colors to achieve the desired visual results when printing a book.

Color Bar (Color Guide): A color bar is a guide printed on the edge of press sheets used by the press operator to adjust color variations prior to and during the printing process.

Color Correct: Color correct means to adjust the processed colors on the press to achieve the desired visual results.

Color Separation: Color separations are decomposed color films used to print the individual colors that comprise an image or graphic.

Comb Bind (Comb Binding): Comb bind is a bookbinding process that uses plastic flexible teeth (like a plastic hair comb but with wider teeth) that fits into holes along the edge of the book's pages to keep them together.

Composing: Composing is the process of setting copy into type.

Contents (Table of Contents): The contents are a listing of the chapters and subchapters of a book, including page numbers.

Co-Op Advertising: Co-op advertising allows a publisher to advertise with other publishers in a catalog, for example, to reduce the cost per ad.

Content Editing: A content editor strengthens the authorial voice and addresses organization, completeness, and the overall quality of the writing.

Continuous Tone: Continuous tone refers to illustrations and photos that have not been screened and contain gradients or varying shade tones.

Contrast: Contrast is the measure of light to dark tones in an image.

Copy: Copy is the written content of a book.

Copy Editing (Copy Editor): A copy editor addresses and corrects the grammar, punctuation, spelling, **style, and consistency of a book.**

Copyright: Copyright is a set of exclusive rights provided to authors of original works to protect them from infringement. Copyright does not protect ideas, but it does protect how those ideas are expressed.

Copyright Page: A copyright identifies the copyright holder of a book. It is found in the front matter.

Credit Line: A credit line is a line of text that identifies the copyright source for material used in a book.

CreateSpace: A Print on Demand platform owned by Amazon.

Crop Marks: Crop marks are small marks or lines on press sheets that identify where the paper is cut to the book's finished trim size.

Cropping: Cropping is the removal or cutting out of part of an image.

Cyan: Cyan is the color blue, one of the four process colors.

D

Debossing (Deboss): debossing is using a die to create a depression into paper. It is the opposite of embossing.

Dedication Page: A dedication page is a special page in the front matter of a book that expresses gratitude to an individual, group, r organization. When space is limited, the dedication and acknowledgments pages are sometimes combined.

Developmental Editor: A developmental editor works with the overall book concept and direction the writing takes to help an author reach the intended market. As the first step in the editorial process, developmental editing includes manuscript organization, strategies to ensure the writing will be complete, and suggestions for strengthening the overall quality of the writing style.

Die Cut: A die cut is a special tool used to shape or cut paper and other materials.

Digital Proofs: Digital proofs are made from electronic book files prior to color separations. When reviewing digital proofs, an author is able to see how his or her book's text, images, and colors will look when printed.

Distributor: A distributor is a company or individual with in-house sales people or outside regional sales representatives ("rep groups") who sell books to book wholesalers and retailers.

Dot Gain: Dot gain is the loss of detail or the increase in darkness caused by the spreading of halftone dots in the printing process.

Dot Pattern: A dot pattern is the combination of dots, in black and white or color, that make up an image.

DPI (Dots per Square Inch): DPI is the number of dots in a square inch used to create an image.

Dummy (Dummy Book): A dummy is a blank book, complete with cover, that is absent of any printing. It is provided by a printer to show a publisher what the finished book will look like.

Duotone: Duotone refers to printing with two colors that overlap each other, such as black plus a spot color.

DRM: Digital rights management (DRM) is a class of copy protection technologies[1] that are used by hardware and software manufacturers, publishers, copyright holders, and individuals with the intent to control the use of digital content and devices after sale.

E

e-book (Electronic Book): An eBook is an electronic edition of a book, read by a computer or special eBook reading device such as a Kindle.

Embossing (Emboss): Embossing refers to creating a three-dimensional effect on paper using a die. It is the opposite of debossing.

Endnotes: Endnotes are notes from a chapter that are collected and printed at the end of that chapter.

Endorsement: An endorsement is a quote from a person, group, business, media, etc., normally found on the front cover, back cover, or in the front matter of a book, stating positive attributes about the book and/or its author.

Endpapers (Endsheets):Endpapers are two sheets of paper, often printed on one or both sides, that are used to provide a clean finished look to the inside front and back cover of a hardcover (and on occasion softcover) book. Endpapers also help hold a book together. In the front of the book, the endpapers are glued to the first page and inside front cover of the book. In the back of the book, the endpapers are glued to the last page and inside back cover of the book.

Epilogue: An epilogue is a closing statement found at the end of a book.

Extent: The extent is the page count of a book.

F

F&Gs (Folded and Gathered): F&Gs are the printed pages of a book, gathered but not yet trimmed.

Flaps (Gatefold Flaps): For a book jacket, the flaps are a 3-inch to 4-inch extension of the front and back cover, which are folded around the boards. For a softcover book, the flaps are a 3-inch to 4-inch extension of the front and back cover (the cover stock itself), which is then creased and folded over itself. The flaps are where information about the author and the book are printed.

Flood (Flooding): A flood is a complete covering of a printed page or book cover with a varnish or other coating.

Flop: To "flop" means to reverse an image as though holding it up to a mirror.

Flush: Flush means to bring text all the way left or right.

Foil Stamping (Foil Blocking): Foil stamping is embossing with colored foil. The die is commonly stamped onto the cloth of a hardcover book.

Font: A font is a specific style and size of typeface, such as Times New Roman, Verdana, or Bookman, for example.

Footer: A footer is a running head that repeats a line of type at the bottom of a page. It typically repeats the chapter or title of the book.

Footnote: A footnote is a devoted area at the bottom of a page where notes from that page are displayed.

Foreword: A foreword is written by someone other than the author to relay background or explanatory information about author or the book.

Four-Color Process (4-Color): Four-color process is printing using the four process colors (cyan, **magenta, yellow, and black) to produce a full-color image.**

French Fold: A French fold is the where the jacket of a book has been folded to produce jacket flaps and also folded over at the top and bottom to provide a clean finished look.

Front Matter: The front matter comprises all pages prior to the main body text.

FTP (File Transfer Protocol): FTP is the electronic transfer of information, usually book design files, from two networked computers.

G

Galley (Bound Galley): A galley is a pre-published book that is a bound paperback and used for marketing purposes.

Gatefold: A gatefold is paper that has been folded inward from the edges to meet in the center. It typically is inserted between the signatures of a book. The reader unfolds the gatefold to reveal art or other graphics.

Ghostwriting: Ghostwriting occurs when someone writes a book for someone else. This service is performed by a ghostwriter.

Glossary: A glossary is an alphabetized listing, found in the back matter of a book, that defines words, phrases, and expressions used in the book.

Gilding: Gilding is gold leaf or powder applied to the outside edges of a bound book.

Gloss Art: Gloss art is paper stock applied with a shiny coating prior to printing.

Gloss Cover: A gloss cover is a cover that has been applied with a shiny coating prior to printing.

Grain Direction: Grain direction is the direction in which the paper fibers run.

Grayscale: Grayscale refers to varying values or shades of black to white.

Gutter: The gutter is the point at which the paper of a bound book begins to curve sharply toward the center.

H

Halftones (Halftone Dots): Halftones are dot patterns that create the effect of a continuous tone image. The fewer the dots the lighter the area.

Half Title Page: The half-title page contains only the title and not the subtitle of the book. It precedes the title page.

Hard Copy: A hard copy is a physical printout of a book's manuscript during any stage of production.

Hardcover Book: A hardcover or casebound book is bound by boards that are typically paper or cloth wrapped and finished with head and tail bands.

Head and Tail Bands: Head and tail bands are decorative strips of cloth glued at the top and bottom of a book's spine.

Header (Head): The header is a margin at the top of page that spotlights a title or message.

House Stock (House Paper): House stock is a selection of papers frequently used by printers. It is purchased in quantity at discounted prices and often results in a publisher receiving the best deal possible.

I

Imprint: An imprint is a subsidiary of a publishing company usually purchased or developed to serve specific niches.

Index: An index is a list of words at the end of a book that guides a reader to the specific pages on which subjects appear in the main body of the text.

Independent publishing: The majority of small presses are independent or indie publishers, meaning that they are separate from the handful of major publishing house conglomerates, such as Random House or

Hachette. The term 'indie publisher' should not be confused with 'self publisher', which is where the author publishes only their own books.

Initial Print Run: The initial print run is the first printing of a new book.

Interior Graphics: Interior graphics are any images such as photographs, charts, diagrams, drawings or art that appear in a book.

Introduction: Introduces the material that is covered in the book. Here the author can set the stage for the reader, and prepare them for what can be expected from reading the book.

ISBN (International Standard Book Number): An ISBN is your publishing "social security number." It is a string of numbers that identifies your book, e-book or audiobook, as well as your status as the publisher or not.

K

KDP(Kindle Direct Publishing): is Amazon's e-book publishing platform

Kerning: Kerning is changing the distance between characters. It is useful for adjusting the text while designing a book.

Keyline: A keyline is a shape, usually a box, used as a placeholder for photographs, drawings, art, etc.

Keywords: Keywords are researched single words or phrase used to generate traffic to a website.

Knock-Out: A knock-out is the masking of an image.

L

Lamination (Laminate): Lamination is the application of a thin plastic coating to the cover of a book or jacket that helps prevent scuffing while enhancing the colors.

Landscape: Landscape is a book format in which the book is wider than it is tall.

Line Editor: A line editor addresses the author's voice as well as grammar, punctuation, spelling, and consistency. He or she may also make suggestions regarding character, plot, dialogue, and pacing.

Literary Agent: A literary agent represents an author to a publisher. The agent negotiates the publishing contract on behalf of the author and typically earns a 10 to 15% commission.

M

Magenta: Magenta is the dark purplish-red color among the four main process colors.

Make-Ready: Make-ready is the final phase in which a book is ready to go on press.

Manuscript (MS): The manuscript is the unedited book as written by the author.

Marketing (Book Marketing): Book marketing involves a comprehensive overview of your potential book sales and promotions activities.

Mass-Market Paperback:A mass-market paperback is an inexpensive paperback book typically printed after the book has experienced success as a trade paperback book.

Margins: Margins are areas outside of the designated printed area.

Matte Art: Matte art is paper that is coated with a dull surface.

Mock-Up: A mock-up is a rough (and sometimes partial) visual concept for a book's design and/or packaging.

Moire (Moire Pattern): A moire pattern is an undesirable wavy pattern found in a printed image. It is caused by scanning a previously printed halftone and then printing it again with more halftones. The result is a double set of halftones or "dots-over-dots."

N

News Wire Distribution: News wire distribution is the circulation of stories among various media.

Niche: A niche is a targeted market of a particular topic. The tighter the niche the more focused the market.

O

Offset Printing: Offset printing is the traditional and most common book printing method. It is the process of pressing rollers coated with ink onto the paper.

On-Demand Printing: On-demand printing is a digital book manufacturing process that allows one book at a time to be printed and bound.

On-Demand Publisher: An on-demand publisher sells editorial, design, marketing and other packages, and prints and ships books on-demand.

Opacity: Opacity is the amount one can see through a sheet of paper.

Orphan: An orphan is the short ending of a paragraph at the bottom or top of a page.

Out of Print (OOP): An out-of-print book is one that is no longer available from the publisher or through its distribution channels. A publisher will have no immediate plans to bring the book back into print. Some authors' contracts stipulate that after a book is out of print the author may request that the rights be returned to him or her.

Over Run: The overrun are the number of copies printed over the requested amount. 5% overrun is typical. Overruns are typically priced less per unit than the main print run.

P

Page Count: The page count is the total number of pages in a book, including front matter, back matter, and all blank pages.

Pagination: Pagination is the organization and numbering of a book's pages.

Pantone: Pantone is a company that provides the standard color-matching system for designing and printing.

Page Proofs: Page proofs are printouts of a book's paginated pages just prior to finalizing the files for printing. They're used to make final checks before a book goes to the printer. They're also used for indexing.

P-CIP (Publisher's Cataloging-in-Publication): A P-CIP is a block of descriptive information, typeset in a specific format, that is found on the copyright page of a book. A P-CIP is used by libraries to catalog books for reference purposes.

PDF (Portable Document Format): A PDF is a common independent document platform created by Adobe. It can contain text, graphics, drawings, etc., and is often used to print pages of a designed book for editing.

Perfect Bound (Perfect Bind): A perfect bound book is a softcover book where the edge of the spine has been applied with glue and the cover wrapped around it.

Photo Credit: A photo credit is a credit line given to the photographer. It typically is found next to the photograph or on a credits page.

PLC (Paper Laminated Cover): A PLC is paper that has been glued and wrapped around the boards of a casebound book. Depending upon the design, it may or may not need a jacket. For example, the PLC may be printed in color with the title of the book alone and then jacketed or printed in full color without **a jacket.**

Podcast: A podcast is a series of audio or video broadcasts for downloading to a personal computer or audio player.

POD: Print of Demand

Portrait: Portrait is a book format in which the book is taller than it is wide.

Preface: The preface is an introduction written by the book's author to explain why or how the book was written. It precedes the foreword in a book.

Prepress: Prepress is the transition of a book design to readiness for final printing.

Printing Plates (Plates): Printing plates apply ink to the pages of a book during the printing process.

Print-on-Demand (POD): Print-on-demand is a digital book manufacturing process that allows one book to be printed and bound at a time.

Print-Ready: Print-ready means the book's design files have met all criteria for commencing the printing process.

Print Run: The print run is the total number of books printed at one time.

Process Colors: Process colors are the four basic colors that produce a full-color image. The colors are cyan (blue), magenta (red), yellow and black.

Proofs: Proofs are provided by a printer as a final check before printing.

Proofreader (Proofreading): A proofreader looks mainly for correct grammar, punctuation, and spelling. The proofreader also may catch errors made during the interior layout process and before the manuscript is finalized for printing.

Publication Date (Pub Date): The publication date is the date when a book is expected to be stocked in **stores and reviews are expected to begin to appear.**

Publicist: A publicist promotes a book and its author through various services, from writing press releases to scheduling book signings.

R

 Remainders: Remainders are a publisher's excess stock or slightly damaged books. They often are sold to third-party remainder dealers for a fraction of the retail price. Remainder dealers then sell quantities of remaindered books to various retailers. CIROBE is the largest trade show for remainder dealers.

Rep Group: A rep group is a group of book salespeople who sell a publisher or distributor's books to retailers. Each rep group covers a specific region, such as Northwest, Southeast, etc., on an exclusive basis.

Resolution: Resolution is the quality of an image as measured by its DPI (dots per inch).

Returns: Returns are books that are returned to the publisher or distributor in exchange for a full refund.

RGB: RGB stands for red, green, and blue. These are the three primary colors in which we view an image. They are converted to the four process colors (CMYK) for printing a book.

Royalty (Royalties): A royalty is a percentage of a publisher's sales of a book that is paid to its author. 8%-10% is a typical royalty on the retail price. Escalating royalties may be negotiated based upon benchmarks on the number of copies sold. Some publishing contracts calculate royalties on "net receipts" (the amount the publisher actually receives).

Royalty Advance: A royalty advance is a negotiated amount paid to an author prior to publishing a book. Royalties from the sale of the author's books are deducted from the royalty advance until it is earned out.

Run-On: A run-on is the number of copies printed over the requested amount. A 5% run-on is typical. Run-ons are typically priced less per unit than the main print run.

Running Head: A running head is a repeating line of type that appears at the top of a page. It typically repeats the chapter's name or the title of the book.

S

Saddle Stitch: Saddle stitch is a bookbinding method that uses staples.

Sans Serif: Sans serif is a typeface that does not have small strokes at the ends of individual letters.

Self-Mailer: A self-mailer is a mailing piece usually used for advertising, sales, or promotions-that can be mailed without an envelope.

Self-Publishing: Self-publishing is the process in which an author publishes a book without the involvement or controls of a publisher, vanity press, on-demand publisher, or other third party.

Sell Sheet: A sell sheet is a single-page document that is used to inform sales representatives about a forthcoming book. The contents also may be used as a BLAD ("book layout and design" brochure) and for other marketing pieces.

SEO (Search Engine Optimization): SEO is the process of naturally raising the visual profile of a site, usually by employing high-demand keywords or search phrases.

Separations: Separations are decomposed color films used to print the individual colors that comprise an image or graphic.

Serif: Serif is a typeface that has small strokes at the ends of individual letters.

Sheet-Fed Offset Printing: Sheet-fed offset printing is a method of printing books in which the paper is either made or cut to the exact size needed.

Signature: A signature is a large printed sheet that when folded becomes a group of pages in a book. The book's signatures are then gathered and bound to make a finished copy of the book.

Slipcase: A slipcase is a special printed or cloth-wrapped box used to enclose a book. Slipcases are generally used for special edition books.

Slush Pile: The slush pile contains unsolicited manuscript submissions to publishers.

Small Press: A small press is a company that publishes books to niche markets.

Social Networking: Social networking allows users to create a profile and form communities on special sites. Examples of social networking sites include Facebook, MySpace, Ning, Tumblr, and Twitter.

Special Sales: Special sales are books sold to non-traditional bookstore markets in large qualities at large discounts. Examples include gift stores, clubs, mail order companies, and other catalogers.

Spoilage: Spoilage refers to books that are not sellable at the end of the printing process.

Spot Color: A spot color is a single color printed on its own.

Spot UV (Ultra Violet): Spot UV is used to highlight specific printed areas of a book's cover.

Spread: A spread refers to the left and right pages of an open book.

Stet: A stet is a notation used by an editor or proofreader to indicate a correction he or she did not intend to make.

Stock: Stock is the paper used to print books. A house stock is one that a printer inventories regularly.

Style Sheet: A style sheet is a document an editor uses to follow the grammatical and other editorial rules established by the publisher.

Subsidiary Rights: Subsidiary rights are found in publishing contracts. They include foreign language, film and television, paperback, audio, book club, serial rights, and other rights. "Second serial rights" follows publication.

Subsidy Publishing: Subsidy publishing is the sharing of publishing costs between the author and the publisher. Arrangements include dividing responsibilities for the various services as well as requiring the author to purchase a specific number of copies.

T

Table of Contents (TOC): The table of contents lists the sections and chapters of a book, along with their page numbers.

Tear Sheet: A tear sheet is a page removed from a newspaper or magazine to show and to prove that an advertisement or review was printed.

Testimonial: A testimonial is a quote from a person or group, typically found on the front cover, back cover, or in the front matter of a book, testifying to the accuracy or positive attributes of a book and/or its author.

Title Page: The title page contains the book's title and subtitle and often the publisher's name and logo.

Trade Book: A trade book is one that has been published for the general retail market.

Trap (Trapping): To trap means to print one ink over another ink.

Trim Marks: Trim marks identify where the sheet will be trimmed.

Trim Size: Trim size refers to the vertical and horizontal measurements of a book's finished size.

Typeface: A typeface is a set of fonts that represents a complete set of characters that form a type style family.

Template: A template is a standard layout used by a graphic designer to design a book, a book cover, marketing and promotional materials, etc.

Tints: Tints are the shade of a particular color.

Tip-In: A tip-in is a special page or group of pages inserted into a specific location in a book prior to binding.

Tissue Overlay: Tissue overlay is a transparent paper tipped into a book to protect a page with artwork on it.

Trade Paperback: A trade paperback is a softcover edition of a book that is published prior to the book's publication as a mass market paperback.

Trim Size: The trim size is the final size of a printed and bound book.

Typesetting: Typesetting is the interior design process of a book.

U

 Unsolicited Manuscript: An unsolicited manuscript is one that an author sends to a publisher without requesting prior permission.

UV Coating: UV coating is a liquid applied to a book's cover that is cured with ultraviolet light. It is used to protect the cover and enhance its colors.

V

 Value Added: Value added is a way to increase the perceived value of a book to the buyer by adding additional features. Examples include colorful tip-ins and special binding. Books also may be paired with other books and products to increase value.

Varnish: Varnish is a clear liquid applied after the book cover has been printed to protect the cover and give it a glossy finish.

Vanity Press (Vanity Publisher): A vanity press is a publisher that requires the author to pay for all of a book's publishing expenses. In return, the author receives a royalty and may have to relinquish his or her book rights to the vanity press.

Virtual Book Tour (VBT): A virtual book tour is an online "blitz" promotional campaign for a book. The tour may include teleseminars, podcasts, webinars, radio interviews, guest blog writing, and other tactics for reaching target audiences over a specific time frame.

W

Watermark: A watermark is an image or pattern in paper that is added during the paper manufacturing process to identify the manufacturer.

Webring: A webring is a group of websites centered around a particular theme.

Webinar: A webinar is an interactive online seminar.

Web Offset Printing: Web offset printing is the process of pressing rollers coated with ink onto a continuous roll of paper.

Wire-O: Wire-o is a binding process that winds circular double-wire strips through holes that are punched along the binding edge of a book.

Wholesaler: A wholesaler provides books to retailers. Wholesalers purchase books at discounts from publishers and then sell them to retailers for a profit.

Wholesale Book Distributor: A wholesale book distributor represents publishers by actively selling their books into retail channels.

Woodfree: Woodfree is paper made from chemical pulp. The process involves the chemical breakdown of wood fibers to change the paper's characteristics to reduce yellowing.

www.ingramcontent.com/pod-product-compliance
Lightning Source LLC
Chambersburg PA
CBHW051836250726
48659CB00005B/1872